I0459395

Pieces
of Me

A WOMAN'S STORY COLLECTION

HANNA OLIVAS
Along With 8 Inspiring Authors

ISBN: 978-1-968061-76-0

DEDICATION

by Hanna Olivas

"To Every Woman Who Has Ever Lost Herself and Found Herself Again."

To the women who were told to be quiet, and instead chose to roar. To the ones who have carried the weight of the world on their shoulders while still managing to smile for their children, show up for their friends, and rise after every fall.

To the women who have cried silently in bathroom stalls, whispered prayers into the void, and dared to hope anyway.

To the broken-hearted, the bruised, the healing, the whole, and the women still becoming, this book is for you.

This book is dedicated to the pieces of us we thought we had to hide. The parts that once made us feel ashamed, afraid, or too different. The wounds we carried in silence.

The dreams we buried to keep peace.

The fire we dimmed to make others comfortable.

The truths we swallowed so we wouldn't be seen as "too much."

Pieces of Me is not just a collection of stories. It's a reclamation. It's a rising.

It's a reminder that nothing we've lived through has been wasted.

We dedicate this book to the women whose stories were never written down.

To the grandmothers who raised generations with their strength but were never celebrated.

To the mothers who sacrificed themselves in the name of love.

To the daughters growing up in a world that still tries to tell them

how they should look, think, and act.
To the sisters, soul-friends, and healers who carried others before themselves.

You are the reason this book exists.
Your voices. Your battles. Your bravery.

We honor the young woman just learning to trust her voice.
We honor the elder who knows her worth and no longer asks for permission.
We honor the woman who has stumbled and is still walking.
We honor the woman who is starting over again.
We honor the woman who never gave up even when no one was cheering her on.

This book is for the warriors in hiding.
The nurturers who never stop loving.
The visionaries who see more.
The phoenixes who rise again and again and again.

This book is for the pieces of us that broke and the hands, hearts, and hope that helped us put ourselves back together.

This is for the pieces that remain tender.
And the ones that became stronger in the fire.
This is for our mothers.
Our daughters.
Our sisters.
Our friends.
And our former selves.

To the women who wrote in these pages, thank you for your truth.
To the women who read these words, thank you for seeing yourself here.
To the women who still think their story doesn't matter oh, but it does.

We see you.
We hear you.
We are you.

So this one's for you.
Every single piece of you.

With All My Love,
Hanna Olivas

TABLE OF CONTENTS

INTRODUCTION

by Hanna Olivas

Why This Book Had to Be Written, and Why You Need to Read It.

There comes a moment in every woman's life when she asks herself "Will I tell the truth, or will I stay silent?"

This book was born from that moment.

It was born in the stillness of 3 a.m. tears.
In the courage it takes to leave a toxic job, a broken relationship, or a suffocating belief system.
It was born in the hospital rooms.
The boardrooms.
The living rooms where mothers teach their daughters what strength really means.
It was born in stories that demanded to be told even when it was hard.

Pieces of Me A Woman's Story Collection was created to hold space.
To hold you.
To honor the sacred act of telling a story that the world might not yet be ready to hear, but needs to.

Each woman in this anthology gave a piece of herself.
Not just to be seen, but to let you know that you are not alone.

You'll read stories of survival, of rebirth, of breakthrough.
You'll walk beside women who've faced unimaginable losses and somehow kept walking.
You'll hear from women who were underestimated, overlooked, and told "no" only to come back stronger.

You'll see the world through the eyes of women who've lived through racism, illness, grief, abuse, betrayal, reinvention, and rediscovery. And you'll see what it looks like to rise anyway.

This book does not offer perfection.
It offers permission.
Permission to feel.
Permission to hurt.
Permission to heal.
Permission to take up space.
Permission to be messy and magnificent at the same time.

As you read, I hope you pause to reflect on your own story.
Not just the highlight reel, but the behind-the-scenes.
The forgotten chapters.
The moments you survived but never acknowledged.
I hope this book becomes a mirror for your soul.
A reminder that even when you felt invisible, you were always worthy.
Even when you were silent, your story mattered.

This is not just a book for women, it's a book for humanity.
Because when women speak, the world changes.
When women are heard, healed, and held, generations are transformed.

You hold in your hands a book that was created in truth, wrapped in love, and released into the world with wild, radical hope.

To the woman reading this now
This is not a coincidence.
You are here for a reason.
You are part of this story too.

So turn the page.
Feel every word.
Let it move you, shake you, wake you, and remind you

You are a woman worth writing about.
You are a woman worth reading.
You are a woman whose story can change the world.

Welcome to *Pieces of Me*.
We're so glad you're here.

With All My Love,
Hanna Olivas

FOREWORD

by Hanna Olivas

Written by a Woman Who Knows What It Feels Like to Be Silenced, and Chose to Speak Anyway.

If you're holding this book, it's because somewhere in your spirit, you know that stories hold power.
Not just the big, sweeping, triumphant stories, but the quiet ones too.
The stories written in tears.
The stories whispered in the dark.
The ones that only ever lived in a woman's journal until now.

Pieces of Me is more than a book. It's a movement.
It's a brave act of visibility in a world that has often overlooked women's voices, especially those who don't fit the mold.

When we first envisioned this collection, we knew one thing for certain, Women are walking stories.
Living testaments of love and loss.
Of rising from ashes.
Of finding faith in the unlikeliest places.
Of choosing themselves, even when it costs them everything.

This book came to life because we believed in the sacredness of telling the truth.
Not the polished version.
Not the social media-friendly soundbites.
But the raw, real, sometimes unfinished truths of women from all walks of life.

And oh, what a gift it's become.
Every chapter you're about to read is a mirror.
A mirror reflecting the joy, rage, heartache, humor, and hope that

lives inside each of us.
You'll meet women who have walked through hell and found heaven in healing.
You'll meet women who dared to dream, who dared to leave, who dared to speak.

These stories are not just theirs, they're ours.
And that's what makes this book so powerful.
It's not about being perfect.
It's about being real.

I remember when I first read the early submissions.
I cried. I laughed. I paused to breathe.
I felt seen in ways I hadn't expected.
Not because every woman's experience mirrored mine, but because her strength resonated.
Because her words healed something inside of me.

This collection reminds us that we are never alone in our experiences, even if we often feel we are.
There is nothing more healing than shared truth.
There is nothing more powerful than a woman standing fully in her story.

If you are a woman who has been silenced
Read this.
If you are a woman who has silenced herself:
Write your truth on the margins of these pages.
And if you are a woman who has found her voice:
Use it. Loudly. Boldly. Authentically.

We live in a world that benefits when women stay quiet.
That ends now.

To every woman who contributed to this anthology, thank you for your vulnerability, your wisdom, your grit.

To every reader, may these stories awaken something in you. May they challenge and comfort you in equal measure.

And may you find your own piece of truth reflected in these pages.

Let this book serve as a love letter.
To the parts of us that were once lost.
To the pieces that have been found.
To the pieces that still ache.
To the pieces we are learning to love.

Let it be your reminder:
Your story matters.
Your voice is needed.
And you, dear woman, are never too much.

This is for you.
This is from us.
This is *Pieces of Me*.

With All My Love,
Hanna Olivas

Hanna Olivas

Founder and CEO of SHE RISES STUDIOS

https://www.linkedin.com/company/she-rises-studios/
https://www.facebook.com/sherisesstudios
https://www.instagram.com/sherisesstudios_llc/
www.SheRisesStudios.com

Author, Speaker, and Founder. Hanna was born and raised in Las Vegas, Nevada, and has paved her way to becoming one of the most influential women of 2022. Hanna is the co-founder of She Rises Studios and the founder of the Brave & Beautiful Blood Cancer Foundation. Her journey started in 2017 when she was first diagnosed with Multiple Myeloma, an incurable blood cancer. Now more than ever, her focus is to empower other women to become leaders because The Future is Female. She is currently traveling and speaking publicly to women to educate them on entrepreneurship, leadership, and owning the female power within.

Erica Elliott

WarriorHeart Healing Hearts, LLC
Counselor. Coach, Author, Speaker & Consultant

https://www.linkedin.com/in/erica-elliott-ms-lpc-b90911150
https://www.facebook.com/warriorheartxo
https://www.instagram.com/warriorheartxo
https://msha.ke/warriorheartxo
https://linktr.ee/WarriorHeartxo

I possess a Master's Degree in Counseling Psychology and have invested over three decades in my career as a Licensed Counselor, Certified Brain Health Coach, and Certified Health Integrative Medicine Professional. My expertise encompasses a broad spectrum of therapeutic approaches, such as Neurobiology, ADHD and Neurodiversity, Somatic Therapy, Energy Medicine, NLP, CBT, RET, EFT, TFT, Theology, EMDR, the Gottman Method, alongside Mindfulness and Meditation. I am an international acclaimed author, speaker and spent over a decade in the military. I am the owner of WarriorHeart Healing Hearts where I champion a comprehensive healing philosophy that harmonizes the mind, body, and spirit. I help individuals clear up the mess to discover their MASTERPIECE using a combination of healing modalities to rapidly rewire for success! Throughout my career, I've had the privilege of helping thousands of individuals, viewing my work not merely as a profession but as a calling. I am truly passionate about empowering others to grow, heal, and soar, unlocking the incredible life that God has always envisioned for them. Having navigated my own share of trials, traumas, and triggers, I deeply understand that healing flourishes through compassionate relationships. Together, we cultivate resilience and vitality, transforming legacies. Like iron sharpening iron, if you're looking for support or just want to connect, you were destined for greatness! Be Blessed and Be a Blessing!

A Journey of Resilience: Finding Light in the Darkness

By Erica Elliott

On an old dirt road in the tranquil expanse of Oklahoma, my childhood unfolded along the banks of the North Canadian River, surrounded by a sprawling farm. This picturesque setting featured grassy pastures, fruit trees, ponds, creeks, and dirt roads that wound for miles before finally meeting the smooth pavement of civilization. As a young child, I found immense joy in the simple pleasures of the many things rural life had to offer—casting my line into the river, climbing trees, swinging in the rafters of the barn, and engaging in playful hunts with my BB gun, even though my grandfather firmly believed that girls were not meant to hunt. While there were countless aspects of country living that brought me joy, I often felt constrained by societal expectations, as if I were being molded into a shape that didn't quite fit my true self.

When people hear tales of growing up in the countryside, they may conjure images of a serene, idyllic life filled with tranquility and joy. However, my experiences were far from conventional. One particularly memorable Christmas, when I was just six years old, I received an enormous box labeled "From Santa Claus." My heart raced with excitement as I jumped up and down in eager anticipation of the surprise within. However, my elation was swiftly extinguished when my grandmother delivered a devastating revelation: that gift was not from Santa Claus, but rather from my biological mother—a woman I had communicated with frequently over the phone but had never been told she was my mother. My grandmother's words struck me deeply: "Santa Clause would never get you something like that. Your mother didn't want you and that's why you're here."

In that heart-wrenching moment, my innocent perception of family and belonging crumbled into dust. A part of me never felt like I fit in.

The emotional scars left by such revelations ran deeper than any physical punishment could inflict. I struggled with the haunting notion that perhaps I was never wanted by anyone. This feeling shadowed me throughout my formative years and I even dove deep into this during counseling to heal the abandonment that plagued my heart. Yet, amid this emotional upheaval, I found solace in the unwavering love of my great-grandmother, who lived next door, and an aunt who would later become my foster mother. Their warmth enveloped me, providing a sanctuary of comfort during a time when chaos seemed to reign supreme. Additionally, my neighbors (whom I often refer to as my Godparents because they taught me so much about God), who took me to church, introduced me to a community that radiated acceptance, kindness, and a sense of belonging. In those moments, I began to catch glimpses of God's unwavering presence and unconditional love.

The departure of my great-grandmother marked a crucial turning point in my life. At just eight years old, filled with feelings of abandonment and isolation, I cried out to God in desperation. I questioned the very essence of His love and existence, wondering why I was left to endure such suffering. As I lay in bed that night, a profound sense of peace enveloped me, as I felt a gentle assurance whispering within my heart: "I will be your Father. I love you, and I have good plans for you." Although my circumstances remained unchanged, that moment ignited a flicker of hope within me that would guide me through the darkest of times.

School, however, presented its own set of challenges. I grappled with reading difficulties and impulsivity, often finding myself in trouble for excessive talking or for being unable to maintain my composure in class. I remember one time so clearly that I and a boy in class competed to see who could get the most spankings. I don't remember who won; however, I do remember getting 11 licks with the wooden paddle. I vividly recall the principal saying to me that day, "Erica, I know what your family is like and what you are going through, but you don't have to be a product of your family." Those words resonated deeply within me, like a piercing of my soul. Though I wasn't sure what he meant, it sparked something deep in me. A desire to break free from the constraints of my upbringing and forge a different path for myself.

As the years unfolded, I faced a multitude of transitions. I began going to California to live for the summer, which, though exciting, new, and sometimes really fun, also brought its own trials with a different cultural aspect of fast-paced city life. My biological mom had married into a Hispanic family, which in many ways was fun, vibrant, and loud, yet also had some dark sides. It was always tough when I left, and I often felt like I had to switch personas to fit in because the culture was so different from one another. I always had the constant presence of God in those whispered prayers.

In one year, around 5th grade, I moved three times, one to spend the summer with a great aunt in Illinois. Then, a dramatic move to the bustling city of Chicago. This change was both exhilarating and intimidating, as I encountered a vastly different environment filled with new experiences. Yet, amidst the chaos, I sought refuge in the church and forged new friendships that provided me with a sense of belonging. Still, the shadows of my past lingered, and I wrestled with feelings of inadequacy and the longing to fit in.

Despite these challenges, I found that God's presence was a constant source of strength. His love provided me with the resilience I needed to persevere through difficult moments, including conflicts with my family and struggles at school. I often recalled the warmth of God's teachings, which illuminated my path during times of confusion and despair.

As I journeyed through grade school, a troubling new struggle emerged as I began to grapple with an eating disorder. Teased by an uncle and classmates at school, I found myself ensnared in a web of negative thoughts about my body and self-worth. When a family member casually mentioned anorexia and bulimia, it planted a seed that spiraled into a battle I would face for years. The internal struggle would ebb and flow, weighing heavily on my heart until I finally confronted it head-on in my early twenties, embarking on a dedicated journey toward healing all of my past.

In my quest for self-improvement, I made a solemn commitment to work diligently in school, motivated by my aunt and uncle's promise of a horse if I succeeded academically. I discovered a newfound passion for learning, and my grades improved as I became more focused and dedicated. Yet, the road was fraught with obstacles; feelings of fear and confusion continued to weigh heavily on my heart.

Throughout high school, I actively participated in a variety of extracurricular activities, including band and sports, which brought me immense joy and a sense of belonging. I embraced my innate talents, particularly in public speaking, where I competed in 4-H events and earned awards for my efforts. However, the shadows of my past still loomed large, and I often grappled with my identity and self-worth.

Upon enlisting in the military, I felt a renewed sense of purpose and direction. I remember very clearly at the age of twelve, when I was reading my Bible, God laying on my heart that I was to be a counselor and minister. I felt a divine calling so deep it brought peace—an aspiration that was now coming to fruition. God's guiding hand was evident as I navigated the challenges of military training, and I excelled despite grappling with ADD that I didn't know I had at the time. It was during this period that I learned about my condition, which eventually helped me understand myself better and discover strategies to manage it effectively.

Living with ADD presented its challenges, but it also gifted me with numerous blessings. My insatiable curiosity and love for learning fueled my desire to explore a wealth of tools and techniques aimed at self-improvement. I immersed myself in studying various strategies, eager to enhance my life in every possible way. I not only absorbed this knowledge but also actively tested these tools in my own life, which proved to be immensely beneficial. This hands-on experimentation not only fostered my personal growth but also enriched my practice as a counselor, as I eagerly shared these insights with my clients, empowering them on their journeys toward healing.

As I entered into adulthood, I was determined to break the cycle of struggle that had plagued my family for generations. When my daughter reached the age of nine, she began experiencing significant difficulties in school, often expressing feelings of inadequacy by saying she was "dumb." I was certain that she had never heard such negativity from me or anyone else, which only deepened my resolve to help her. Together, we explored various tools and techniques, even incorporating supplements recommended in Dr. Daniel Amen's book *Healing the Seven Types of ADD*. However, when those strategies fell short, I took her to see a psychiatrist, where she was ultimately diagnosed with ADD.

The diagnosis was both a relief and a new beginning. The psychiatrist prescribed her medication, and within just a few days, she reported feeling completely different—more focused and capable. In a matter of weeks, her grades began to rise, and within a few months, I could see a remarkable transformation in her demeanor. She started to express feelings of self-worth and confidence, proudly declaring that she felt so much better about herself. As she matured, however, she began to express her dislike for the medication, feeling that it inhibited her ability to engage in the dreamy, creative thoughts that defined her vibrant personality. We always took breaks from the medication on weekends or when school was not in session. Then, eventually, she only took them for testing and reverted to supplements.

Through this experience, I witnessed firsthand the power of the right tools and support in overcoming challenges. I have pursued extensive training in ADD, learning about the seven distinct types of ADD, and I highly recommend anyone who is struggling with ADD or has a family member with ADD to learn more about the different types and tools that help each.

In addition, it's important to understand the parts of the brain that are affected by ADD. Research indicates that individuals with ADD often experience differences in the prefrontal cortex, which governs executive functions such as attention, impulse control, and decision-making. Additionally, the basal ganglia and cerebellum may exhibit variations that impact motor control and coordination. One of my favorite acknowledgments of understanding ADD by Dr. Amen was his stating that a person with ADD, when we observed it in a SPECT scan at rest, showed better blood flow to the prefrontal cortex than if they were asked to focus on something, which then showed less blood flow. He went on to say, so it's like the person puts on the gas and the brakes at the same time when they're trying to concentrate. I think it's very important for anybody dealing with ADD to understand this has nothing to do with intelligence but everything to do with blood flow and a neurobiological issue in the brain. With the right tools and medications or supplements, a person's life can be immensely improved, allowing them to function at their highest level and raise their self-esteem as well.

Not only because of my job working as a trauma counselor, but also because I myself went through traumatic things as a child, I specialized in PTSD (Post-Traumatic Stress Disorder). There are certain aspects of PTSD symptoms that are similar to ADD symptoms. PTSD has profound effects on the brain as well, linked to alterations in brain regions such as the amygdala, which is responsible for processing fear and emotional responses, and the hippocampus, which plays a crucial role in memory formation. Individuals with

PTSD may experience heightened levels of anxiety and emotional dysregulation, often resulting from traumatic experiences.

While both ADD and PTSD can significantly impact an individual's life, they differ in their origins and manifestations. Understanding these distinctions and the brain's response to each condition has empowered me to provide better support for myself, my daughter, and my clients.

In my adult years, my relationship with God deepened even further. I dedicated much of my time to ministry in lots of areas. My love for the Lord has always been profound, encompassing my heart, soul, and mind. God has been my constant, the unwavering love that picks me up when my world feels like it's falling apart, holding me close and reminding me that I am never alone. Guiding me when I'm lost or unsure.

During my graduate studies, I was fortunate to have a mentor who specialized in ADD. This relationship opened doors to new insights and techniques that profoundly transformed my life. I learned to embrace my uniqueness and view my challenges as opportunities for growth. God had placed the right people in my path at the right moments, steering me toward a future filled with hope and purpose.

Today, I stand as a testament to resilience, equipped with the understanding that God has been my steadfast companion throughout my journey. My life narrative is one of healing and transformation, where I have unearthed the gifts that lie within me. I have come to realize that it is not our circumstances that define us, but rather how we respond to them. I strive to use my experiences to empower others facing similar challenges, offering hope and encouragement to those who feel lost.

As I reflect on my life, I see the intricate tapestry woven by God's hand—a story of struggle, triumph, and unwavering faith. I am profoundly grateful for every experience, as each has shaped me into the person I am today. My story is not merely my own; it stands as a reflection of God's boundless love and grace—a reminder that even in the darkest moments, He is there, guiding us toward the light of hope.

Through my extensive training in ADD and PTSD, I have had the privilege of helping thousands of individuals navigate their own paths. I firmly believe that with the right tools and strategies in place, anyone can achieve success in life.

I want to share a few of my favorite tools for individuals with ADD:

1. Mindfulness and Prayer: Engage in daily mindfulness practices along with heartfelt prayers to center your thoughts and foster a deeper connection with God. This practice can help alleviate anxiety and enhance your ability to focus.

2. Structured Routines: Establish a consistent daily schedule that encompasses dedicated time for work, rest, and spiritual reflection. This structure can create a sense of stability and significantly reduce feelings of overwhelm.

3. Visual Aids: Utilize calendars, planners, and visual reminders to keep track of tasks and responsibilities, aiding in organization and effective time management.

4. Task Breakdown: Divide larger tasks into smaller, more manageable steps. Celebrate each accomplishment to maintain motivation and a sense of achievement.

5. Physical Activity: Make it a priority to engage in regular physical exercise, which has been shown to profoundly help. Nature has a calming effect that can help clear the mind and improve focus.

6. Creative Expression: Explore various creative outlets, such as writing, music, or art, to channel energy positively and foster a sense of self-expression.

7. Healthy Nutrition: Maintain a balanced diet rich in nutrients that support brain health. Ensure you stay adequately hydrated to enhance your focus and energy levels throughout the day.

8. Technology Tools: Leverage apps designed for time management and organization, such as reminders and productivity tools, to help streamline your daily tasks.

9. Support Networks: Build a supportive network of friends, family, peer groups, or coaching groups where you can share experiences and find encouragement in your journey toward personal growth.

10. Therapeutic Techniques: Seek guidance from mental health professionals or coaches who specialize in ADD. There are numerous tools to help with coping strategies and insights for managing symptoms effectively.

I encourage you to reflect on these tools with an open heart and a sense of curiosity rather than harsh self-judgment. Identify the areas where you excel and those that could benefit from further development. Understanding yourself and others can foster compassion and empathy rather than condemnation.

Throughout my extensive career as a counselor and coach for over thirty years, I have witnessed the transformative power of choice and self-awareness. Each individual is amazing and wonderful with unique gifts and talents and has the potential for meaningful change, but only if they are willing to embark on a journey of self-discovery and growth.

Remember, you are not alone, and the transformation you seek is within reach. Let's embark on this journey together—your masterpiece awaits, guided by faith and the promise of a brighter future. As a brain health coach, I help people clear the mess to discover their Masterpiece using Neuropsych evidence-based tools to rapidly rewire for success! When you're ready to soar, and I know you are, let's connect.

You may want to check out my newest book, which is filled with neuroscience and tools to help you live a more blessed life—*Breath of Heaven: Manifesting God's Way*. Plus, later this year, I will have a new book out—*We Repeat What We Don't Rewire - It's a Program*. You can connect with me and find free resources in the link below. I am always adding new tools and links. Be Blessed and Be a Blessing!

Nadia Sheikh

Finance Professional

https://www.facebook.com/nadia.sheikh.464624
https://www.instagram.com/sheikhnad2025

Nadia Sheikh was born and raised in Calgary. She has lived in six different cities across Canada. She has been volunteering since the age of 10 and had early exposure to many different areas from Leadership to Politics at early age. She had started mentoring and tutoring from an early age as well. She had achieved a blackbelt at the age of 15 had participated in both Nationals and Alberta Winter Games. In her professional life she has worked in different intermediary companies ranging in different industries from Finance to Insurance to Medical to Auto, to Technology and Manufacturing to Distribution and to working on retail, to travel and tourism to working with people with disabilities and also taught boxfit and beginners bootcamp.

Getting to Know Me

By Nadia Sheikh

A lot of people ask me where my interests started and what it is that I haven't done. To be honest, as I was going through the different stages of my life, I didn't really think that what I have done till this day would have happened the way it did. As I was going through the motions, the only thing I could do was try to reach my goal, and that was it.

I am definitely a big advocate for kids and to teach them as much as you can, or give them exposure, because a lot of my dreams, interests, and passions all started from my childhood.

I loved my childhood so much that after I went through my trauma and began healing from it. The healing process had brought back my inner childhood. Not that I lost it in the first place, but it had me turn back internally to bring that part of me out again. I am also grateful for it because a lot of the people who knew me as a child can tell you that I am the same person that they knew, just with a lot more baggage and experience; however, I am still the same girl they knew when I was a child.

So, let me start my childhood story and how my imagination and my love for my hobbies and interests started. As a toddler, before I could speak, the first show that I started watching was *Sesame Street*. My parents always used to tell me that I would never miss an episode, or if I wanted to watch it, I would point at the TV to have them put it on. The other shows that I would watch would be *She-Ra, He-Man, Care Bears, Mr. Rogers' Neighborhood, Reading Rainbow, Today's Special, Read Along,* and *Magic Ring*. With *Read Along*, I learned how to sound out words and phrases, so I started reading at the age of 4.

The show *Magic Ring* used to be one of my favorite shows. There was this robot named Matilda, this boy named Jeff, and this girl named

Vicky (I am shocked that I still remember the names). So, what I loved about it was that as I was watching the show, I would actually copy what they were saying by repeating the words and imagine that I would be going along on adventures with them. In this show, they would either end up in a park, a zoo, or any other interesting place. The best part of watching it was that I was so engrossed in the show that it felt like I was there with them.

I was also an avid reader. As a kid one of my favorite things to do was to go to the library and take out piles and piles of books. I used to read from *Where the Wild Things Are*, the *Curious George* series, *Berenstain Bears*, *Dr. Seuss* books, *Sweet Valley Twins*, *Baby-Sitters Club*, T*he Secret Garden*, the *Anne of Green Gables* series, Christopher Pike's books, all the Roald Dahl books, to the *Lord of the Rings* series. Non-fiction books from Ancient Egypt, History of Greece, and reading on the planets and dinosaurs. So, I had read all these types of books during elementary school as well.

When I was a kid, I used to live in Calgary, Alberta. One of my favorite things as a kid was to try to get lost in one of our national parks, called Fish Creek Park. My friends and I would ride on our bikes in Fish Creek. We would pretend to be explorers and the first people to find a new place. The park covered all four quadrants, so we would try to get lost in the park. Or we would use our imagination to pretend we were discovering a New World. The other thing we would do when we played in the fields was lie down on the grass. During the day, we would lie down on the grass and watch the clouds. We would also watch the formation of the clouds to try to figure out the shapes of the clouds. At night, we would do some stargazing and try to figure out the constellations. Till this day, cloud watching, stargazing, and just lying out on the grass are some of my favorite things to do.

Elementary school was actually one of my favorite childhood memories and has been one of my favorite places where I used to like to be. The reason for that was that we had some of the best teachers, and I would say one of the best environments I've been in. I felt safe, secure, and just liked the atmosphere, the kids in the school, the teachers, as well as the people who used to work in the office, and the principal. This is where I had actually picked up a lot of my imagination and basic skill sets for today.

This was the place where they had taught us to be respectful towards one another. There was no pushing, yelling, arguing, swearing, or fighting allowed. Even the teachers had to be respectful towards the students as well, and vice versa.

I remember when I was in Grade 1, there was this boy who got to eat in class. The rest of us asked why. Then, the teacher explained to us that the boy needed to eat to keep his sugar up. So, that was my first exposure to learning about diabetes. We got to learn about arthropods: we created a habitat with tinfoil and dirt and got to learn all about them. That was one of our first exposures to bugs. We had a pet python snake in our science class. We would all circle around the glass cage and watch the snake eat the dead mouse. We all watched as the snake ate the mouse and how it moved down the snake's body. Then, my teacher asked if we would be interested in touching the snake. We all said yes. So, before our teacher took out the snake, we all lined up beside each other. Before he brought out the snake, he double-checked with us to see if we would like to touch the snake. We said yes. He brought out the snake, and he had put the snake in all our hands. That was my first time touching and holding a snake.

In Grade 2, one of my friends' dads had actually won the city election and became the Mayor of Calgary. So, he had come to our school to talk about politics. It was in Grade 2 that I had my first exposure to politics. My friend's dad ended up being the mayor of the city from the time we were in Grade 2, and had stopped running when we graduated from high school.

In school, I was one of the kids who would be the first one to finish our school work in class. We had gotten so good that the teacher had decided to have a couple of us work on a special project, and once we had done our project, we would have to present it in front of the class as a presentation.

Once we had completed our projects and had presented them to the class, our teacher was so impressed by our projects and our presentation that she had actually published our work in one of the newsletters. So, you can say that was one of my first published works. Our English class teacher would have us write stories. My mom used to love my stories. My first story was actually a character that was an apple, and the adventure that it went on. My teacher loved my story. She had published my story in our school storybook. That was my first published story ever. I was so proud of that.

In elementary school, I used to be a part of the Patrol Team (Crossing Guards). We had to remember a pledge in order to become a part of the team. I remember we had a police officer come to observe our team to see how we performed our duties. After we were done, he had us gather around his car. We were nervous at first because he gave us a serious look. From that look, we were a little scared. Then, he gave us a smile and handed us his evaluation. When we all took a look, we could not believe our eyes. We had received a perfect score. After he handed it to us, he also gave each of us a bag of chips with chocolate. He shook our hands and said, "Congratulations"! We were all so excited and giddy. After he left, we were just jumping for joy and were chanting "We rock!"

In my Elementary school days, I had also joined the Leadership Club. The type of activities we ran and organized were bake sales, Candy Grams, collection of goods for people who were less fortunate, collecting items to put in shoe boxes for the Non-Profit Organization, such as Operation Shoebox. Another part of our mandates was to relieve secretaries during their lunch. We also used to enjoy using the PA systems to make announcements.

Another thing I used to love about my school was that they used to teach us about the Indigenous Culture and the environment, and how to protect it. In relation to the Indigenous Culture, not only did they teach us about the different tribes that used to live across the country, but they also taught us firsthand. They would have guests from the First Nations come in. They told their stories and also performed traditional dances, and they also taught us some as well. They also taught us about the significance of the land, the totem poles, and how each one of them has stories, and how they pass the stories down from generation to generation.

Environmentally wise, they had taught us about Mother Nature and how pollution affects it. About recycling and planting trees. Not only did my school teach us about culture and environment, but they were also very passionate about it when they taught us. That is probably one of the reasons why I am passionate about the causes to this day.

One of the other things that I loved about my elementary school was the diversity of the field trips we went on. It made it fun, memorable, and I had an interest in many different areas. The trip to the science centre and planetarium had piqued an interest in the way science works. The planetarium has always been my favorite. Because of that particular trip, it has always kept my interest in stargazing and looking out for meteors, constellations, planets, shooting stars, comets, and the northern lights.

Another thing I loved about my elementary school was when our class needed to read two books that had been released. We actually got to meet both of the authors. We were all very excited to see them because we really loved the books, and at the same time, we got to get our books autographed. That was my first exposure to authors.

For music class, we used to sing a couple of songs from this one French singer. Because he was one of our favorite singers, we actually got to meet him at the recording studio and go into his studio. While he was in the studio, he was actually recording the song. So, he called us in and asked us to sing as his backup.

That was the first exposure I had to recording a song.

One thing I loved about our music teacher was that she had us singing songs from *Phantom of the Opera*, *Les Misérables*, *Cats*, and *Joseph and the Amazing Technicolor Dreamcoat*. Because my music teacher had us sing these songs, I fell in love with theatre.

When I was in school, I was not the typical girl. My mom would call me a tomboy just because I used to love playing sports. In the gym, I would always love to play soccer, volleyball, capture the flag, ultimate frisbee, baseball and belly baseball, basketball, and floor hockey. I used to play all these sports during gym or recess. I enjoyed all of the sports so much that it became almost like second nature while playing them. Some of the teachers had asked me if I played any of the sports on a team outside of school. I told them no. I was proud when my gym teacher told me that I was a natural athlete. To this day, I still can hear him telling me that.

My dad had wanted to see how I would like martial arts, so he had put me in a beginner's class to see how I would like it. When I was in the class, I enjoyed it. When that particular class session had finished and the stripes were being handed out, I was the first one to be called out. As my sensei was handing out the stripes, he had told me he was very proud of me, and I was so happy when he told me that.

So, when my dad saw that I enjoyed the classes, he then put me in a Karate School. During the time we were put in the school, we would go three to four times a week. We also participated in tournaments and camps. I would say, out of all the accomplishments I had, this would have been my best accomplishment. During my martial arts career, there was never a girl of my age. So, in tournaments up to green belt, I would have to fight with guys. From purple and onwards, I would have to go two to three age categories up. When I had gotten my black belt, not only was I my sensei's first student to get a black belt, but I had also set a new standard for the head of the Japan Karate Association.

I had my own class at the age of 15. I have won many awards, have competed in the Nationals, and have won two bronze medals in the Alberta Winter Games. We also used to do demonstrations in malls and had also done a demonstration at halftime for the local basketball team in Calgary. As I reflect back on my life, which just involves my childhood, I still cannot believe a lot of the things that I have learned and picked up.

That is one of the reasons I advocate so hard to teach kids and to build their character when they're young, to build self-confidence in themselves. The main thing is to teach them to have confidence in themselves, love themselves, and most of all, to put faith in the up above. The foundation starts at the childhood level.

Joyce Ayers

Create Your Life After Divorce
Coach

https://www.linkedin.com/in/joyce-ayers-79893b85/
https://www.facebook.com/joyce.ayers.395669/
https://www.instagram.com/awakenwellnesswithinreach/
https://createyourlifeafterdivorce.com/
https://createyourlifeafterdivorce.com/rewilding-after-divorce-1

Heartbreak can feel disorienting, even for capable women. After years of packing her dreams into boxes and waiting for someday, Joyce Ayers learned how easily a woman's voice can disappear in the busyness of caring for others and compromise. Drawing on neuroscience, somatic therapy, and spiritual wisdom, she now transforms heartbreak into a catalyst for self-discovery and renewed purpose. Joyce's work is informed by her own journey—she has known the silence of disconnection and the hard-won freedom of reclaiming one's voice. Whether leading intimate retreats or one-to-one mentorship, she invites women to excavate the truth beneath their pain, reweave their narratives, and step into sovereign wholeness. Clients learn to calm the nervous system, reframe limiting narratives, and architect futures anchored in authentic values, achieving health and a return to self-direction. Joyce is a Certified Conscious Uncoupling® Coach, Master NLP and Hypnosis Practitioner, and energy healer. Connect at Joyce@CreateYourLifeAfterDivorce.com.

Reclaim Your Dreams

By Joyce Ayers

I thought I was in the driver's seat, but my husband held the GPS. At first, it felt like an adventure; eventually, a surrender to the life we had. I agreed to job opportunities in other states, making the most of the next "adventure" while picking up the pieces as we moved along. Not having dreams of my own, I was very accommodating and went with the flow, wherever that would take me next. That's just what you do in a marriage, right? Surrender and adapt.

As we settled into yet another move, I discovered aerobics while four months pregnant, which seemed doable given everything I had already been juggling and would just be for me. I even trained as a fitness instructor and worked towards becoming an aquatics instructor. Then came the announcement that we would be moving as soon as baby #2 was born. Eleven days later, boxes packed, we set off on another adventure. The silent "go with the flow" was becoming too familiar. If my dreams fit in a moving box, how big were they?

At home, I tended to the family's needs, including Chantel, our German Shepherd, and kept things running like a well-oiled machine. I lived in a bubble, on mute, so I could keep focused on the task at hand. I never stopped long enough to consider how unhappy I was becoming. Just like I had seen my parents do growing up. Did I have a voice? Of course! Did I know how to use it... NO!

When you settle into the mundane routine of taking care of kiddos, the house, errands, and playdates, it doesn't leave much time and energy to focus on yourself, UNLESS you decide to make YOU a priority. Many years later, I have come to know this wisdom and can assure you, YOU are a priority right now. Start allowing your voice to speak to you and what you truly desire for yourself. Making YOU a priority is non-negotiable!

Exploring a life for myself outside of my family would have to wait until someday. Even though I had always looked for my own adventures, trying new things, taking courses, and making new friends, this stage of my life was all hands on deck, tending to the many family needs and my husband's business demands.

Yet under my calm, efficient exterior, I had forgotten dreams put on hold of a Psychology degree. So, instead of full-time education, I created a large vegetable garden, which I named my "Peaceful Oasis," and considered multiple greenhouses that would grow organic food for restaurants.

That summer, my garden became my sanctuary. I prepared the soil in the raised beds as I had researched and carefully chosen which plants would go well together. I studied companion planting, biodynamic rhythms, and cultivated a garden of love and tenderness. Near the end of the season, I discovered I loved growing plants, not growing a business. My garden helped me harvest my sense of self, and parts of me began to blossom.

My husband never asked me to disappear. I did that well enough on my own. I had trained him that my needs and dreams didn't matter and that I could take care of myself. Just like I trained the cucumber vines to grow up the trellis, I began to retrain my thoughts and soul to honor myself.

When you listen with your soul, it whispers truth and love. The mind is what shouts for attention to feel safe and worthy. Make time for the quiet moments so you can begin to hear your soul speak.

It took a long time to retrain my soul to lead. Just before I married, I had a sense that I wanted to keep my name. I liked shifting traditions and thought it was a good idea. As I shared my idea with some happiness and innocence, my husband stated, "If you don't take my name, there's no wedding." It wasn't a request. In a split second, I silenced that part of myself and decided what he wanted mattered more than what I wanted. If you've ever broken your own agreement to keep plans moving forward, you know the defeated "okay" that follows.

This pattern was the script I lived by for years, and my happiness dutifully followed this script. I didn't have a strong enough reason for the things I thought I wanted to do, so I deferred to others who did.

When we don't have a strong WHY for what we want and need for ourselves, others will decide for us. This shrinks us into living life through others, never truly feeling in charge of our destiny..

Life was like being on a ship pulling into port, knowing you won't be staying: four relocations, three daughters, two funerals, and a 24/7 start-up while feeling like a single mom for five years. So, I decided I needed support and not just the physical kind. There were other moms out there who helped me keep my sanity and feel supported.

In my attempt to do something for myself over time, I found a lifeline with yoga, and the studio I attended was offering an embodiment workshop. Yoga taught me that your body never lies, and in that studio, mine was urging me to attend. We stood in similar poses to yoga, yet very different. My body felt like it was being plugged into a power source, which I hadn't felt in a long time. I became reconnected to myself and signed up for their practitioner training right away. I may not have gone back to continue my education at a college, but I was going to continue learning my way. I felt this was my calling, and the only permission I needed was from myself.

When you feel that powerful YES in your body, trust it as the truth. No need to explain, justify, or rationalize your next action. Just a solid "I'm doing this" determination, so get out of my way or support me. Your body language can act like a flashing neon sign that advertises your decision has been made.

During the embodiment training, one of the lessons was a pose called "open." As the facilitator guided us to lie on our backs, he asked us, "Where in your life do you feel truly supported?" Before any thoughts appeared, years of unshed tears spilled down my cheeks. My life had all the basics covered: marriage, home, trips, opportunities, but what I needed most of all was emotional support.

In that moment, I saw the cost of my role as caretaker: ignoring my own needs disconnected me from myself and others, leaving an empty feeling inside because I didn't think I could count on anyone to really be there for me in the ways I needed.

As I continued with my new educational path, I added Coaching, NLP, and Hypnosis. NLP rewired my self-talk, hypnosis untied the knots, and Conscious Uncoupling let me bless the goodbye. My "agreeableness" lessened, and I went on a quest to find happiness.

My new tools helped me self-regulate in challenging moments so I could see situations from a new perspective. It's very enlightening to witness yourself in old ways and wonder how you could have possibly lived that way. I started loving myself as my new self, setting boundaries, and creating a life I loved.

My husband felt the shift in me and wanted to understand what had changed. Not so much me, but its impact on him. We did the typical therapy, read books, attended marriage classes, but couldn't seem to find a new way to relate to one another.

People relate to one another because we are similar. When you choose to show up differently, they may not be able to relate to you any longer. That's when you have a choice to stay in the past as you were, or take the high road and see if they follow you.

After several years of drifting further apart, we mutually agreed to part ways, and I found a new freedom within myself. It was liberating!! There were fewer and fewer times I showed up small, invisible, and silent. Listen to your body's response when you shrink yourself, and ask what a more empowered, loving YOU would do instead.

Those first few steps you take can be scary and intimidating once you're out of your comfort zone, which provides a false sense of security, love, and acceptance. Yet this next step will bring more aliveness to your life that fills you with excitement and purpose.

Shortly after my divorce, I began the tedious process of changing my married name back to my family name. It felt uncomfortable at first reclaiming an old identity, and I really didn't have a strong sense of who that was. I was like a toddler learning how to navigate my emotions while not understanding them.

Think of emotions like radio stations. They each have a frequency to tune into. A soft hum lets you know you've drifted off course—like agreeing to help with a project when the whole house needs to be managed every day. Screeching static means apply the brakes and take a quick assessment.

I learned to tune into my emotions to navigate uncharted waters: sometimes, a walk would help stabilize my emotions, or journaling to explore a boundary needed, even an embodiment check-in for a clear "yes/no."

Having a deeper understanding of yourself through your body and emotions provides the confidence you need to course correct when you default back to an old pattern that doesn't "suit" you. The NLP methods I learned were like a compass pointing me down a new road better suited to my dreams. Conscious Uncoupling coaching helped me say goodbye to my marriage with gratitude and love. Staying grounded when stress threatened to take the wheel kept my GPS on course.

As I strengthened my own foundation and business, women began reaching out for help. Guiding them through divorces, career pivots, and late-life reinventions showed me that my earlier silence was never a weakness—it was my inner strength waiting for the right timing to bloom. With every client breakthrough, my confidence solidified the wisdom that our choices, not our circumstances, decide the story we live.

If you want to choose a new story to write, you don't need a five-day retreat in the mountains, though a retreat is a good way to start.

Start now with two simple practices that fit into everyday life.

#1 **Emotion Check-In**: When a feeling surfaces, pause. Name it—anger, envy, regret—and ask, *What is this emotion telling me?* Meet the answer with compassion, then ask what your soul truly needs right now. Feelings are like a compass; ignoring them takes you off course.

#2 **Future-Self Snapshot**: Close your eyes for sixty seconds and picture the most grounded, authentic version of yourself. How does she stand and breathe? What does her voice sound like—clear, warm, a little playful? Imagine her routine: the calls she accepts, the projects she declines, the way she says yes only when she means it. Open your eyes and tackle the next task as if you are already living in her body. Repeat every day. Neuroplasticity will do the rest.

Practicing these micro-shifts slowly becomes a confident way of being. You start choosing friendships that nourish your new identity instead of draining you. Seek out adventures of your own that feed your soul. You may even find yourself experiencing a full-body, unrestrained laugh once in a while that brings back the playful child inside.

Some days, the old programming may try to sneak back into your life. Check in with your emotions if the signal is clear or full of static and make the necessary adjustments.

Transformation isn't linear, but it leaves footprints so you can track how far you've come by how quickly you course correct.

Understand that your patterns and choices sculpt your life and the results you get. If you keep silencing yourself, life will mirror that silence through unfulfilling relationships, unexplored talents, and a chronic static hum of "will it always be this way?" But patterns can be rewired and chapters written in your voice as the author.

Real change begins with a whisper and may feel awkward at first. Know what's most important to you and stand by it, appreciate who you are and your contribution to others, and meet your needs like no one else ever could—even if your voice shakes.

Speak your truths aloud and protect them with boundaries that seem uncomfortable at first but will soon fit like a glove. Hear the silence within and feel your heart beating, knowing you are connected to a deeper part of yourself. So pause and listen. Tune into your emotional frequency for direction.

When you turn your attention inward, you shift doubt for clarity. You'll start to cultivate courage, acceptance, and love that generate independence, authenticity, and autonomy. When a woman speaks in her own voice, she becomes the inspiration for every other woman to do the same.

So practice being yourself, speaking from your soul. The life you design from this place may surprise you—fewer random acts of people-pleasing and more mornings that start with curiosity rather than dread. And when another woman utters her first shaky "NO," you'll recognize that sound, smiling inside knowing she's about to rewrite her next chapter, just like you.

Together, we steer one another toward our truth, one step at a time.

Joyce Ayers
Relationship & Divorce Coach
CreateYourLifeAfterDivorce.com

Carin LaCount

Dr. Carin M. LaCount
Author

https://www.linkedin.com/in/carin-m-lacount-o-d-354052214/
https://www.facebook.com/carin.lacount/
https://www.instagram.com/dr.carin/
https://www.drcarinlacount.com

Dr. Carin is a mother, an author, and optometrist with a passion to help others see themselves and others in the world. With complete transparency she presents her life's challenges in The Love Liar: A Memoir of Codependency, Narcissism and The Pursuit of Self-Love. She tells us of a childhood tragedy, a life-threatening auto-immune condition and dysfunctional relationships while holding herself accountable to unconditionally love who she is and the decisions she's made. Since publishing her memoir, Dr. Carin has continued to heal from codependency, fiercely breaking the generational pattern of toxic conditional love. She feels strongly about understanding her childhood so as to not pass on this legacy of pain to her children. She called Wisconsin home her whole life until moving with her kids to Austin Texas in 2021. She continues to nurture that most important relationship with herself, ensuring her children receive the invaluable gift of self-love.

The Question That Changed Everything: How One Moment of Motherhood Sparked a Lifetime Journey to Self-Love

By Carin LaCount

"What would you ever do if I died?" my very exasperated mother asked me one evening when I had asked her to kiss all my stuffed animals before she tucked me into bed. With the question on her lips and hands on her hips—you know that way mothers do to let you know they're waiting—she cocked her head and smiled at her six-year-old child as if she hoped I would appreciate her.

While she kissed Marius, the big orange bear near my pillow, she left the others alone and moved on to plant a kiss on my forehead. She then backed toward the door and quickly blew one more kiss my way while I lay confused about her question. I had no idea a mother could die, let alone know what I would do if she did.

* * *

Days later, my father took my mother to the E.R. for a severe headache.

I've often wondered, before the brain aneurysm took her life, whether she had any idea she would never see me again. Did she have any thought as to how much her question would haunt me for the rest of my life?

At her funeral, I asked my father how to pray. Informed as I was by the shock of her passing, while still confused as to what death was, I realized I had an answer for my mother's question: I would cry. I would wonder for weeks where she was and why she wasn't coming home. For years to come, I would see her face in crowds, long for her in the presence of my friends' mothers, or mourn her again when I'd see the smile of any older woman with short, curly, dark brown hair.

I would also accept and deeply integrate this unreasonable thought that she was unhappy with me and left because I didn't give her the love she needed in the moment with an answer to her question.

* * *

My ceaseless mulling over this exchange has led me to the conclusion that she was simply overwhelmed. She had four other children, including my baby sister, to attend to along with a never-ending checklist, and was looking for *someone* to appreciate her efforts.

Like so many of us, my mother never learned the power of self-love. She didn't understand how loving oneself could relieve one of the need to seek validation from others, unprepared or incapable of giving it. If she were in a self-loving place, she would have had compassion for herself in that moment and not have had the desperate longing to be loved, seen, and appreciated by me.

She would never have asked me the question that haunted my whole life.

This is one of those defining moments in life that are so often brushed off as inconsequential. However, once we can release the fear that has us downplay its significance and truly look at it, the love we bring in can be an elixir to healing.

I've had to do this for myself after a lifetime of troubled relationships. Despite being Catholic, my father couldn't explain to me how to pray, nor did my asking prompt him to consider that I might need professional support to understand that I did nothing to drive my mother away. My empathic, child-logic sensed that my mother needed something from me, but no one thought to teach me that what she needed was not for me to give to her, but for her to give to herself.

As I've come to figure this all out, I believe that understanding and teaching our children about self-love is the only spiritual practice a child needs. It is the only necessary foundation for healthy mental and emotional development. This way, we are not driven to depend on our children to love us. When we can love ourselves, this gives us the space to unconditionally love those who need us. When we can love ourselves, it allows us the opportunity to teach our children that they need not give us love in the form of hassle-free behavior and obedience.

Imagine your life choices if, from a young age, you never had the idea that you needed to sacrifice your needs and desires in order to make someone else happy and receive their love.

* * *

I don't fault my parents. I don't even fault my stepmother, who came along less than two years after my mother's death and reinforced the idea that love had conditions. The generations before us were never taught that when we respect, cherish, and unconditionally love ourselves, we naturally pass that on in the most healthy manner of parenting.

Instead, my parents were taught what they taught me: love comes from others and must be earned. You must obey your parents and make them proud or suffer the consequences of not having your basic emotional needs met. If you want anyone to love you, you must either give to them what they need to be loved, or manipulate them for the love you need.

We are taught to be codependent or narcissistic, and when we are in fear that we are not getting love from another in some fashion (either attention, money, compliments, favors, etc.), parents and society teach us in increasingly clever ways how to accept counterfeit love, as so very few understand true, unconditional love.

For the next fifty years after my mother's death, I consistently chose the path of giving to others in the hope that they would love me. In other words, I became a codependent people pleaser, a pattern that started in the last moment I can remember with my mother.

In her question to me, asking what I would do if she died, she demonstrated a need for me to see that I needed her. In her mind, that validation of my needing her was the equivalent of love.

With my mother's innocent question, she powerfully demonstrated how one obtains love, driving me to slowly give up my life—almost to the death—as I became the best people pleaser I could possibly be to receive love from others.

And still, love continued to elude me.

* * *

Codependency in relationships is a common plight of the people pleaser. I was desperate for love and would accept any unsupportive, unloving, or outright abusive behavior in relationships, romantic or otherwise. I was often taken advantage of by others because I would rather give everything I could of myself than lose their misguided "love" and attention.

This was how I'd come to marry a man who was also incapable of loving himself. Neither one of us was taught self-love by our parents, and we were, therefore, poised to neglect that most important lesson for our own kids.

Until I initiated our divorce.

Then, I began the slow understanding of how I'd been lying about love my whole life because, based on my childhood, I didn't know any better.

* * *

In the 27 years my husband and I had been together, there was a part of me that suspected I deserved better. It was a very quiet, loving part of me that was bullied into submission by the loud, frightened part of me. The part that insisted he didn't mean to insult me, he didn't intend to consistently ignore my needs in favor of his own, and that he simply didn't understand my very complicated heart because, well... my parents showed me that no one could.

I had no reference from my own upbringing that his ersatz love wasn't the real thing. He didn't know love any more than I did. Rather, we each operated from our ingrained coping mechanisms—his being narcissism and mine being codependency—to get love from one another in the only way we knew how. His method was manipulative emotional abuse, coercion, and lies, while mine was martyrdom as I kept giving until my life literally depended on my learning to stop that pattern and love myself.

Ulcerative colitis was my cross to bear. I'd had many flare-ups of the autoimmune condition since my marriage, and in 2013, I was sick again. This time, I needed a blood transfusion for all the blood I'd lost through my ulcerated colon.

It was the same night my husband needed a night out to see a band two hours away, but the threat of my asking a family member to take care of me—thereby giving witness to his blatantly selfish attitude—gave me a win in our battle for conditional love.

He had to deal with me, but he made sure to let me know how much of a burden I was in every way he could, from complaining about his boring day to bitching that we didn't have enough money to fix his car's squeaky brakes because I was too sick to earn a paycheck.

I wondered how I had gotten to this place where I was married to someone who not only didn't care about me, but could think of nothing other than how much of a burden I was to him when I was too sick to take care of myself.

On the way home from the hospital that night, the quiet, loving part of me stood up to the bully of fear inside of me. That night, anger broke free from the ever-present self-love in my heart and obliterated the need for my husband's indifferent, totally conditional love. I decided there was nothing loving about accepting abuse.

A week later, I told him I wanted a divorce and began to unearth the lies we'd both told about love.

* * *

Sadly, blood transfusions don't cure you of people-pleasing, and my husband wanted nothing to do with a divorce. Even though I knew that wasn't because of his love for me, I allowed him to persuade me to find us a therapist to save the marriage "for the kids."

My husband had no intention of seeing his role in our dysfunctional relationship. He only wanted me to figure out how I was the problem. My decision to hold off on separating and engage in counselling delayed my self-love progress by another eighteen months as I became confused about what was best for my children.

* * *

On the courthouse steps after the divorce was final, I naively believed myself to be free of whatever that marriage was. I told myself I had outgrown him and it was time for me to move on. It never occurred to me that I still had much to heal, or that it had anything to do with my mother.

Three months later, a text came to me from an unknown number.

"Hi Carin, you should be happy you got rid of that asshole."

I knew my ex-husband was dating. I assumed this text came from some jilted lover he'd started seeing, but I was only half right.

I've always said that the best thing my former husband ever did for me was cheat on me. Not only did his infidelities reward me with the much-needed validation that "codependent" me needed from others for the divorce, but they also woke me up from my smug reverie that I'd been through the worst of it.

My ex-husband's affairs highlighted for me just how concerned I had been about showing him love so that he would love me, while I was oblivious to the fact that he was incapable of loving me. I had made myself sick trying to handle everything for him and the kids while neglecting my own needs.

This was how my mother's self-love challenges were passed on to me. Her innocent need for me to acknowledge her worth, given the simple ask I made for her to kiss my stuffed animals, is something we've all done in some manner. It seems harsh to assign a lifetime of grief to her glib comment days before her unexpected death, but that's how I've come to understand that this world works. We each have countless such comments that we've made or received that could either go unnoticed or change the course of a life in microscopic ways. It's simply how the world goes 'round.

Of course, we cannot control how other people might take our comments, but it is forever in our control to love ourselves. I have learned that when we can love, respect, and validate ourselves, then we have no reason to fear that we will ever be without these life-sustaining necessities. This is how we can leave abusive relationships, and this is how we can own our mistakes to our children and begin to teach them to love unconditionally.

With this self-love as our foundation, we are less likely to make comments that hurt others in ways we never intended.

I am eternally grateful to my parents and my ex-husband for this lesson on self-love. They have indirectly shown me that it is of the utmost importance for how I raise my kids, something that I would never have realized had I stayed married.

Initially, I saw the value in my own healing, but then quickly saw that without doing this work on me, I would simply pass the legacy of heartache to my kids from generations of parents and grandparents unable to find the most imperative of loving relationships with themselves.

* * *

Over the years, I faltered often under the weight of my process. Most dangerously, two years after the divorce, I found myself in an ambulance receiving one of the four blood transfusions that saved my life. The importance of understanding self-love and how unself-loving I had actually been became a life-or-death situation.

Despite all the bubble baths and nature walks I'd taken after my divorce, declaring how much I loved myself, I had to face the fact that my every thought, decision, and interaction was rooted in my codependent patterns. In my arrogant attitude that I "divorced the fucker," and just needed to find true love and move on, I internalized my unloving behavior to such a degree that the ulcers in my colon bled out.

In the ambulance, I reflected on how much effort I had put into explaining to my ex-husband, my family, and friends how much he hurt me. In that moment, I came to realize that my desperate attempt to receive compassion and validation—or love—from others for my pain was because I couldn't give it to myself.

I saw that ultimately I believed I didn't deserve love because my own mother left me for not giving my love in her moment of overwhelm.

* * *

Although I knew my children understood that I loved them unconditionally, I had nearly left them behind on this planet without teaching them how to love *themselves* unconditionally. Without my surviving that illness and continuing to deepen my self-love practice, my precious babies would for sure have fallen into the same legacy of codependency and narcissism that destroyed their parents' marriage. This could potentially have created health issues for them and dysfunction for their own children.

The biggest lesson of my life is that the more self-loving souls on this planet who make decisions based on the love in their heart rather than the fear in their minds, the more peace we will each find on earth. When we choose friends and partners with love rather than fear, and raise our children or mentor others from a place of self-love, there is no telling of the beauty we can create in relationships and in life.

Sneha Jhanb

Mindful Commune
Life Transitions Coach

https://www.linkedin.com/in/sneha-jhanb/
https://www.facebook.com/sneha.jhanb.90
https://www.instagram.com/amindfulexplorer
https://explore.mindfulcommune.com
https://explore.mindfulcommune.com/services-page/

Sneha Jhanb, an author of Indian origin, has lived in the United States with her family for over 18 years. With a background in Engineering, she has expanded her path to include certifications as a Mindfulness Teacher and Sound Bath Practitioner. By day, she works full-time as a Project Manager at a game-technology company, balancing technical leadership with creativity and heart. Outside her professional role, Sneha is dedicated to guiding women through life's transitions— whether in career, relationships, or personal growth. Her work blends ancient wisdom with modern tools like mindfulness, sound healing, tarot, and journaling. Drawing from her own experiences as an immigrant, working mother, and seeker, she creates spaces where women can find clarity, courage, and calm. Sneha believes that transition is not a breakdown, but a breakthrough—and she's here to walk beside those ready to reclaim their voice, purpose, and peace. Her writing and workshops reflect that compassionate mission.

The Sounds That Shaped Me: A Life in Sound, Memory, and Meaning

By Sneha Jhanb

Sound Healing Practitioner and Life Transitions Coach.

Born Into Sound: My Earliest Memories

I was born in India, surrounded by ever-interesting sounds around me.

My mom once told me that when I was born, I stopped crying only when someone turned on the fan, and I could hear the noise around me and feel the air on me. It certainly looks like sounds made an impression on me from very early on.

The most peculiar sound that I remember is the one of my own crying. I remember my sister was trying to record a poem or a song, and was complaining that I was crying out too loud. She was telling me that I should not be "singing" along with her, and that it was her turn.

I remember one of my great-grandmothers making a sound that sounded like "ingya ingya vangya" to mimic my crying.

Ever since I was a little child, I have been surrounded by sounds that have fostered amusement, interest, and a culture of belonging.

My mother and grandmother sang beautifully. The sound of their voices has always been nurturing to me. I remember the devotional song that my grandmother sang every Thursday evening when I visited her in the summer holidays, "A Dutta Aarti."

I remember when my family gathered and made my mom sing, she used to sing a song called "Devaaaa," and suddenly my eyes used to water. I'm not sure why I cried, but I think it is because her voice was always so touching and made me feel so present.

While my dad did not sing, his stern voice was always a voice of knowledge, conviction, and confidence. It was also that of caution and discipline.

Every little voice and sound that I have encountered has stayed with me, tucked away in the corners of my memory like quiet companions. I may not always recall them consciously, but every now and then, often when I am doing nothing in particular, a sound or a feeling will stir something within me. A memory will rise to the surface, vivid and unexpected, offering me a glimpse of a moment I thought I had forgotten. It's as if a piece of my past returns to visit, carrying with it a message I wasn't ready for before, there to teach me something new, to offer comfort, or simply to entertain me in a quiet, reflective moment.

A Street Symphony: Life in an Indian Neighborhood

One of my beloved funny sound memories is the one where my friend Manasi and I are laughing our hearts out as my mom is mimicking a fruit vendor. He used to sell guavas and had this peculiar cry. "Peruuuuuu..." which I can hear even now and chuckle in amusement.

My mom is quite funny and entertaining when she is in a really good mood. Her natural being is the one to enjoy, have fun, and live in the moment. There was another time when I was studying for exams with another friend, Amruta, and I remember almost choking on a gulab jamun (an indian dessert that resembles mini donuts dipped in a sweet sugar syrup) while laughing at mom's fruit vendor mimicry. These moments were few and far between in those busy times, but they left an impression of fun and laughter and joy in me. The joy of living in simpler times, where we needed very little to keep ourselves entertained.

When I lived in India 20 years ago, there used to be fruit and vegetable vendors (and really a lot of other types of vendors) who used to sell their goods street to street on hand-pushed carts. Each of them had a unique voice and a way of calling people out to let them know they were on the street, so people could buy their vegetables and fruits of the day.

People bought what they needed daily, cooked fresh, and never ate stale foods. I remember summer afternoons when the whole day was a procession of various vendors, selling something and always calling out loudly: mangos, guavas, watermelons, bananas, and kulfis (Indian stick ice cream). The corn seller in the rainy monsoon season and chikoos in the winter are also embedded in my memory through their signature calls. My mouth starts watering when I remember those days. That freshness, those sounds, those smells, were something else. I feel like those were simpler times. "Pura vida," like they say in Costa Rica.

And then, there used to be some other people who came once or twice a year but left impressions on me. There was "Kadak Lakshmi," a man who would bring a huge leather belt type of thing along with him and hit himself; a man with a bull who would tell you predictions of your future; an occasional beggar lady who would come wrapped in straps and get sarees and donations from people. They all had peculiar sounds, and just by their cries, I knew who had come onto the street.

Living in India offered a backdrop of noises. The noise of the hustle and bustle was always around us. I always feel the nostalgia of the noises of honking of auto rickshaws on streets, the music my neighbor's car would play (when he backed up to park this car) in the middle of the night loudly blasting "Om Jai Jagdish Hare," the summer birds chirping their hearts out, the crows cawing, the motorcycles accelerating, and the sounds of older aunties hanging out and gossiping in the middle of the day on the corner of the street. There used to be a nightly "gurkha" (watchman) who used to make rounds and make noise with his stick, announcing he was there. I don't believe he was appointed by anyone, but he would also ring the doorbell every Diwali (the Indian festival of lights) for his Diwali fee that he charged for protecting people and watching for everyone's safety.

There were children always playing cricket or other fun games on the streets, friends calling upon each other at the top of their voices from the ground floor to the top floor.

And then, there were some very prominent sounds to hear during the Ganpati festival from the Ganpati pandals (stages) decorated lavishly with lights and other decorations in every street to welcome the Lord Ganesha for 10 days of the festival. The pandals played Bollywood songs as well as devotional songs very loudly. And then, these were blasted again through the loudspeakers during Navratri and Dandiya time. And finally, during Diwali, I remember hearing loud firecrackers.

The Orchestra of Home

My parents' home was always and still is bustling with sounds. In the morning, around 6 a.m., the doorbell ringing starts. The milk guy shows up, followed by the newspaper guy, followed by the guy who cleans the car, followed by the cleaning lady, followed by the cooking lady.

I remember that when I was growing up, there was a beautiful feeling of an air cooler running in the summer. The air cooler provided white noise, and it used to feel so nice and cool to sleep near it. We did not grow up with central air conditioning. There used to be a huge cooler in the living room, and we used to sleep next to it in the summers when the heat was unbearable.

Throughout the day, there was the sound of puja, mantras, the pressure cooker, the news, tennis and cricket on TV, Hindi movies, songs of Kishore Kumar, Lata Mangeshkar, R.D. Burman and others, the phone ringing, the washing machine, and so much more. I find there is always so much auditory overload when I visit India.

Silence and Stillness: My American Soundscape

I moved to the United States of America for my master's degree. The sounds of the past were not just background noises but a backdrop of a culture that I grew up in. They were the music of a slow and sweet life that is now somewhere in the past and does not really exist in my present.

Now and then, I hear the echoes of these voices when I am thinking of India or reminiscing memories with my parents, sister or telling a story to my children of a world that they really cannot relate to. I find the sounds amusing every time I return to India for a visit. Sometimes, I find them annoying, too, as I am not used to them anymore. I mean, who is used to doorbells ringing at 6 a.m. in the morning and disturbing your peace for a bag of milk?

In the United States, I got used to the sound of silence. It is so eerily silent, especially in the suburbs where I have always lived. Everything is so silent that you can hear the sound of your stomach as it growls, or the sound of your breath. You can hear the fridge and the icemaker, or the HVAC noise as it kicks in.

The silence in the United States is definitely contrasting to the noisy hustle and bustle that I was used to in India 20 years ago.

New Sounds, New Anchors

There are no street vendors coming to suburban communities on a daily basis. Rarely does an ice cream truck show up with its peculiar music. No one rings doorbells on a daily basis. Even when people come to your home, you really do not expect a doorbell to ring. People just message these days on WhatsApp or text, and do not meet that often in person. So, it has become rare to even hear a phone ring.

But as life has moved on, I have embraced new sounds. The sound of my children talking, playing, laughing, and even fighting. The sweet sound of my husband when he calls my name. The sound of my new favorite TV shows that I have binge-watched, the sound of country music, the barking of my dog, and the baseball parents cheering. The sounds of friends and laughter when we meet, the sound of my niece and nephew and their cats.

While I do not get to listen to Bollywood music and Indian mantras and devotional music on loudspeakers, there are now enough places to go and enjoy these throughout the year with the family and friends.

There are opportunities to attend concerts, attend MLB and NFL games, and hear different sounds that are associated with those experiences.

And a very American thing that I enjoy is Christmas songs that start playing everywhere as soon as November begins. I look forward to those, and they instill a sense of joy and nurture in me every time I listen to Christmas music. And instead of Diwali, we get to enjoy spectacular firecrackers on the 4th of July.

Listening as a Practice

I have noticed that sound, no matter which of my cultures, Indian or American, has always anchored me to joy and presence.

Yes, there have been enough sounds in my life that remind me of scary times and not-so-fun times, too. And I have learned to work with them and listen to them differently.

Listening is a spiritual practice if you let it. I always ask the question: *What does this sound want to teach me?*

Whether it is a thunder or sweet sound of rain, whether it is an angry voice of a loved one, whether it is a long forgotten tone that creates anxiety, every sound is here to teach us something.

I believe that sound is not just something I hear, but it is something I listen to with intention; it is something I feel, enjoy, and learn from.

Between 2 continents, sound has always been a constant companion. Always bringing me back to breath, always bringing me back to belonging.

The Call Within: Sound Healing and Mantras

Today, I use sounds with more intention. I choose what voices and what sounds to let in, what sounds to learn from, and which ones to let go. As I started learning more and more about using sounds to help me come back to the present moment, I started using sound to help bring connection, community, and belonging back.

I got introduced to Nada Yoga, or yoga of sound, sound healing, and singing bowls, a few years ago. It was the time when I was trying to learn more about different forms of meditation and helping myself find my center. I noticed that something as simple as toning the sounds of chakras can create so much peace and healing in the body. Chakras are thought to be energy centers in our body that help us balance different forms of energies like our health, spirituality, sexuality, belonging, manifestation, etc. I learned to balance these energies using sounds.

The singing bowls reminded me of bells in the churches and temples and helped me find inner peace and calm. They bring about an instant meditative state. I never knew that sound could be so powerful, yet in some ways, it feels like I have always been connected to the power of sound.

Slowly, my relationship with sound has shifted. When I am annoyed by sounds, I question the trigger of annoyance instead of questioning the sound first.

When I am called to a sound, I question if it is pleasing, bringing out a beautiful memory, meditative or uplifting. I have become more sensitive to sounds and try to stay away from negative loud sounds and voices that are not motivating or uplifting to me.

I have started sharing the practice of sound healing not just with myself but with my family, friends, and clients. We have started chanting mantras with intention, learning their meaning, and helping the vibrations of mantras bring their magic into our daily lives.

This has helped me embrace my roots of Indian culture while keeping up with the new-age meditation and healing in America. It has brought peace and mindfulness to me, and also a purpose of helping people use sound as a way to connect more and more with themselves.

It is amusing to me that the girl who once laughed at fruit vendors calling people is now creating her own sounds to bring people back home.

Sound has always been my companion through countries, cultures, heartbreaks, healing, and homecomings. From the cries of fruit vendors on the street to the sacred hum of mantras in my meditation room, each note, call, and whisper has shaped my story.

Over time, I have learned that sound is more than what we hear; it's what we feel, remember, and return to. When approached with intention, it becomes a tool for grounding, joy, presence, and belonging.

As a sound healer, I am fortunate to help people pick up pieces of themselves and bring them back home through the medium of sound. Each tone, vibration, and silence is a bridge, carrying them across thresholds of memory, grief, and longing, back to wholeness.

In these sacred moments, I am not just offering sound; I am offering sanctuary, where the soul remembers itself and the body exhales what it has held for too long.

This is not just my work; it is my prayer in motion.

Sound, Memory, and Belonging

For readers who are interested in beginning their own sacred journey with sound, I am sharing this gentle four-step practice.

Step 1: Pause and Listen

Listen to the sounds around you. Notice different sounds. Name them. No need to judge them as good or bad. Just notice which sounds are closer to you, and which sounds are farther away from you. Practice this for a few minutes daily and let these sounds naturally guide you into stillness.

Step 2: Feel the Sound

Listen to the sounds around you while touching your belly. You can even play bells or mantras and just notice how sounds move inside of you. What effect do they have on your body and mind? How do they make you feel? Do they feel nurturing? Do they make you feel happy? Are they bringing memories? Do you want to shut any of them down?

Step 3: Create Your Own Sound

Hum, sing, tone. See what it feels like inside your body. How easy or hard is it for you to make your own sound? Does your own sound soothe you? Does it bring up emotions? Does it bring up tightness in the throat?

Step 4: Curate Your Sounds

Start finding what sounds soothe you and uplift you. How can you be surrounded by more of those sounds? Turn off the sounds that you do not want around you. Understand which sounds have what kind of effect on you and journal daily to create your own soundscape.

Your relationship with sound is yours to cultivate: moment by moment, memory by memory, mantra by mantra.

Let it guide you home.

Andrea Russell

Founder of Journey to Business Success
Business Implementation & Financial Accountability Coach

www.linkedin.com/in/andrearussell1875
https://www.facebook.com/acrbookkeepingplus
https://www.instagram.com/christianwomenpreneur
https://businesscoach.andrearussellcoach.com/mentor
https://resources.andrearussellcoach.com/home

Andrea Russell is a 2x Best-Selling Co-Author, Business Implementation & Financial Accountability Coach for Christian women entrepreneurs. She helps faith-driven women go from financially stuck and overwhelmed to confident, profitable, and purpose-filled without guilt. Through her honest coaching style, biblical wisdom, and practical strategies, Andrea empowers women to break financial strongholds, price with clarity, and grow businesses that honor God and bless others. Her signature approach helps women stop striving and start stewarding so they can build boldly in faith, walk in financial freedom, and create a business that truly reflects who God called them to be.

From Pieces to Purpose: S.O.A.R. in His Grace

By Andrea Russell

Pieces of Me… God's Grace Is Sufficient for Me

Growing up in church was my entire life. Sunday mornings? Church. Wednesday nights? Bible study. Friday evenings? Youth group. And let's not forget choir practice in between, because if you weren't in the choir, were you even in church?

I was that student who always sat in the front row, turned in extra credit even when I didn't need it, and believed in never just giving 100%, but at least 150%. (Who came up with that percentage, by the way? Because I need them to explain where the extra 50% is supposed to come from.)

Where did that drive come from? Well, for starters, my mother always said, "When you do something, you do it right or not at all." And my stepdad? He had his own version of motivation: "If you start a business and it doesn't work out, close it and open another one until something sticks." Now, that may not be the soundest business advice, but at the time, it made sense.

So, this is my story.

I always knew the right thing to do, just like Apostle Paul said, but knowing and doing are two very different things.

At 19, I fell in love. Or at least, I thought it was love. It was the kind of love that made your heart race, your head spin, and your common sense take a permanent vacation. One minute, I was a church girl with big dreams, and the next, I was holding a positive pregnancy test, staring at it like it personally betrayed me.

And let me tell you, nothing humbles you faster than a church lady giving you that look. You know the one, the "Bless your heart, but you should have known better" look.

To make matters worse, my great love vanished faster than free snacks at a church potluck. Poof! Gone. Just when I had fully embraced the single-mom-to-be life, guess who decided to show up? Eight months later, there he was, all apologies and promises, thinking he could waltz back in like nothing happened. And me? In a moment of divine wisdom, or pure stubbornness, I thought, *Oh, I'll show him!*

So, what did I do? I married someone else. Someone I had only known for a few weeks. (Yes, you read that right. A few weeks.) If there were ever a time for a "girl, what were you thinking?" intervention, that was it.

I went from one bad decision straight into another.

Now, let me pause and say this: If you've ever made a terrible decision and thought, *How did I end up here?*, just know you're not alone. Life comes at you fast, and sometimes, we're just trying to keep up.

Marriage? Oh, it was a hot mess. We had two children, but love was nowhere to be found. We fought more than we laughed, and eventually, the only thing we could agree on was getting a divorce. By the time my daughter was a little over a year, it was over.

And that one decision, a decision made out of hurt and spite, had long-lasting consequences. My children grew up without a relationship with their dad. Not because I didn't want them to, but because he chose not to be there. Out of spite.

For a long time, I beat myself up. I replayed every mistake, every choice, every regret, like a sad movie on repeat. Guilt became my constant companion. I felt unworthy, broken, and beyond repair.

Then, something changed.

I met my now-husband, a man who, like me, had been through his own share of bad decisions and heartache. We both had baggage, enough to fill an entire luggage set, but one thing we had in common? We were both desperately seeking the Lord.

Together, we studied scripture. We prayed. And slowly, I began to understand something powerful:

God still loved me.

He forgave me.

So, why was I still holding onto shame like a security blanket?

When I finally grasped that truth, really grasped it, it was like a weight lifted off me. I stopped beating myself up and started living. Not just existing. Not just surviving. But truly, freely living.

I realized that life happens. We make mistakes. We go against what we know is right because sometimes, we just want to do things our way. But even in our worst moments, God is faithful. He is patient. And He is always waiting for us to come back to Him.

Everything I went through, all the pieces of me that felt shattered, God was putting back together. And now? Now, I help other women avoid the very pitfalls that nearly took me under.

Today, as an author, business implementation and financial accountability coach, I work with Christian women entrepreneurs to overcome the "money is a sin" myth, manage it with wisdom, and grow in faith and profits.

Because let me tell you, if there's one thing I know, it's how easy it is to let life knock you off course.

The world will take little pieces of you if you let it.

Your confidence.

Your joy.

Your faith.

But here's the thing: We get to choose the direction we go. We get to make new decisions. We don't have to let our past dictate our future.

And while we can't erase our past mistakes, we can learn from them. Because the decisions we make, especially when we're young, have a lasting impact. And the consequences? Oh, they are much harder than you can imagine.

But no matter what you've been through, no matter how many wrong turns you've taken, God still has a plan. And when you lean into Him, He will turn it all around for your good. Why? Because you love him.

And that brings me to S.O.A.R.

If you want to move forward, if you want to grow, if you want to step into the life God has for you, then it's time to:

S – Surrender to God's Plan

Let go of trying to control everything. Trust that God knows what He's doing, even when it doesn't make sense.

O – Overcome Obstacles with Faith

You will face challenges. That's a guarantee. But instead of running from them, face them with faith. God will equip you.

A – Align Your Actions with God's Word

Making good decisions isn't just about avoiding bad ones. It's about intentionally walking in wisdom and making choices that honor God.

R – Rise Up and Walk in Purpose

Your past does not define you. Your mistakes do not define you. What defines you is what you do next.

It's time to S.O.A.R.

God's grace is sufficient.

You are not broken. You are becoming.

And every piece of your story, yes, even the messy ones, has a purpose.

So, what will you do with yours?

As you close this chapter, I pray you see your own story in a new light, one full of grace, growth, and God's goodness. The journey from broken to whole isn't always easy, but it's always worth it.

If you're ready to go deeper, into healing, reflection, and peace, I've created something to walk alongside you: a gentle guide to help you process, pray, and grow, one day at a time.

You can grab the *30-Day Journal: From Pieces to Purpose S.O.A.R. in His Grace* and take the next step at your own pace, with faith leading the way.

It's time to *S.O.A.R. in His Grace, From Pieces to Purposes.*

Hannah Darby

Healing with Hannah
Holistic Healer & Grief Therapist

https://www.linkedin.com/in/hannahdarbyhealingwithhannah/
https://www.facebook.com/healingwithhannahdarby
https://www.instagram.com/healingwithhannahd/
http://www.healingwithhannah.co.uk
https://www.accph.org.uk/united-kingdom/martley/therapists-and-coaches/hannah-darby

Hannah Darby GMBPsP SMACCPH is an award winning trauma and grief therapist who helps guide individuals on their personal grief journey. Hannah's unique Kintsgui Method with H.E.A.L.™ approach has been featured in international magazines. Hannah is a General Member of the British Psychological Society, a Senior Member of Accredited Counsellors, Coaches, Psychotherapists and Hypnotherapists, a Reiki Master, a HeartHealing® practitioner, Masseuse and an 2x International Bestselling Author. Hannah founded Healing with Hannah, a unique therapy practice based on her professional and personal wisdom guided by science and spirituality. She guides people on their personal grief journeys with care and compassion. Hannah works with your mind, heart and body to help you find deep healing with soulful integration. Hannah resides in the British countryside with her husband, four cats and two chihuahuas. She enjoys country walks, music and movies. Hannah is a woman of faith.

The Frequency of Gratitude

By Hannah Darby

Life is like a book. A story, our story, that gets written throughout our lives. A new chapter is added every day. We are effectively all the authors of our own lives. We don't get to decide all of our experiences, but we can decide how they shape our future. We get to shape the narrative, we get to be the hero or the villain in our lives. It's up to us to decide how we want our story to unfold.

How do we want our story to be shared?
How do we want our story to be heard?

By unlocking the wisdom in our story, we can make sure the story heads in the direction we want. Ensure that we stay the hero of our story. The creator of our anthology.

If my life were a book, this would be a window into the anthology series of my life. I aim to inspire you that no matter how tough things get, all hope is not lost. You still get to decide how you think and feel about yourself. You get to say how you think and feel about your life experiences. You get to say how you want the readers of your life to see your story. There is a fire inside of every one of us—a drive to succeed, a will for a better life, a dream that needs fulfilling. We all have a mission that at times may seem improbable, but never impossible.

This is important: improbable but never impossible. No matter what you're facing, what you have been through, or what you are about to face, remember that.

There is a strength and resilience inside each of us. This strength and resilience are tested at different points in our lives. By choosing to take your power back. By taking back control of the areas of your life you can, you can ensure you remain the writer of your story, not the reader. You have the power to decide how your story gets portrayed. You have the power to achieve the improbable. You are the author of your story, so own this with pride.

You all have faced challenges in your lives. Some of us more than others. Some of these challenges are small, some are big. Remember, you cannot compare these challenges with others. What counts as a challenge is individual to each and every one of us. Our definitions of big T and little t trauma are all different. Your story is valid, your life is valid.

Come on a journey with me into a part of my story and see how I chose to rise up, fearlessly commanding the cards handed to me with grace and gratitude. I am, after all, the author of my own life.

Life is all about vibrations. Everything in our world consists of atoms; all these atoms have their own energy, vibrating so fast they appear solid. Learning to harness the power in your emotional vibration will transform your life.

All of our emotions have their own vibrational frequency, the Abraham-Hicks emotional guidance scale. Emotions, such as Joy, Gratitude and Forgiveness vibrate at the highest frequency, while emotions, such as Fear, Grief, Guilt and Despair vibrate at the lowest frequencies. What we give out, we also attract—The Law of Attraction, most notably talked about by Dr Joe Vitale in his book by the same name. What we experience in our lives dictates the emotions we experience. But every experience we go through has positive and negative emotions attached to it. A lot of the time, with negative experiences, it is harder to see a positive, but there will be one hidden behind the pain; you just have to search long and hard to find it.

Let me give you an example: finding a positive in the death of my father as a teenager was hard at the time. But over 20 years later, through reflection, prayer, meditation (and HeartHealing™), I can now see how it positively shaped and influenced my life. It guided me onto a healing journey that brought me to writing a chapter in this book that you are reading now, which is not a bad thing at all. I thank you for taking the time to witness a part of my life story.

It is in the quiet moments of reflection and introspection that you can work on raising your vibration. By focusing on those emotions higher in the emotional scale, and not allowing the lower frequency emotions to linger. All emotions have a time and a place. Whatever you feel is valid for you. But allow those feelings to flow like a river, do not build dams with the negative emotions and stop the flow of positive emotions into your life.

How does this work in principle?

I want to share some of my story with you to help bring this idea to life. So you may become the master of your emotions, rather than let your emotions master you!

Life tests us all the time. It tests us to see how we will cope with new challenges, different ways to lower our vibration, and different ways to test our faith. It gives us curveballs. Sometimes, it even comes in with a wrecking ball, usually just when everything seems to be going well. I have had a few of these in my time. Here is one...

I had started a new career in Dentistry, and I had worked as a Compliance Manager all the way to a Specialist Implant Nurse with a Radiography qualification. Not long after obtaining this new post, I was just starting to get my finances in order, finally feeling like I was going somewhere. Then, I started to feel unwell. I had massive swellings in my neck glands, honestly, it was like I had literally swallowed a tennis ball! I had fever, fatigue, malaise, brain fog, nausea, muscle aches/pain, light and noise sensitivity, headaches... I could go on, but you get the idea. I generally felt f*cking awful. I would have some time off and rest, go back to work, and it would all start over again. Each time I had off was longer than the last. Each time the symptoms came back stronger, they came back louder, and they arrived with new friends to join the pain party in my body.

I was no stranger to pain, having broken my back in a life-changing car accident around 10 years ago. I learnt to manage the aftereffects of this accident with physiotherapy, medication and acupuncture. But the biggest help was the art of reframing—reframing the narrative in my mind. Changing the way I thought about pain psychologically, as well as managing it physically. Thinking of pain as my old friend. Learning to live with it rather than fight against it. Honestly, this simple reframe changed my life for the better and still does every single day.

But this was different... The collection of symptoms, the unpredictability of my body, the unknown reason as to why it was happening was a heavy weight to bear. I literally felt like I was drowning. I had test after test, scan after scan, saw specialist after specialist... This went on for over a year, but it felt like 10. A whole year with no idea as to what was going on. A whole year battling unseen symptoms, facing a condition without a name. A whole year feeling like a failure, stressing about letting work down. I literally felt like I had lost the plot completely. Then, finally, I got an answer.

We talk about not labelling everything, that this is not a good way forward. But for me, getting a label to add to my symptoms, a name to call my condition, was a massive turning point. It gave me a sense of peace. It helped me to understand the new me, to give myself the care and compassion I deserved. Whereas before, all I had for myself was guilt and shame. That name was Myalgic Encephalomyelitis/Chronic Fatigue Syndrome, or otherwise known by its abbreviation, ME/CFS.

Even though this is a condition without a cure, there is only symptom management with no guarantee that I will ever go back to the person I was before. I felt a huge sense of relief being able to give my collective symptoms a name. For me, my Chronic Fatigue

Syndrome was brought on by a severe viral infection thought to be Cat Scratch Fever. However, I possessed all the precursors to ME/CFS. If you looked at a profile of who may be more prone to developing this disability, it was like looking in a mirror at myself. So, sometimes I do wonder if God already had this planned for me. I now knew why I was getting worse and worse. If you push yourself, try to do the typical British thing of stiff upper lip, bury it down and just carry on, with this condition, it gets worse and worse. I may never get back to the old me, but I am at peace with this now. This realisation made me put the brakes on fast. My crashes were already terrible, I spent time housebound and didn't want to end up bedbound. So, I had to have a long, hard look at my life. I worked out my priorities and learned to manage my energy as if it were gold: protect it, spend it wisely, plan every detail and prepare for the unexpected. Without your health, you can't have anything else. Your health is your single biggest priority. Don't take as long to realise that as I did. Everything else should be second to our health.

Living this life with all these symptoms takes its toll on many areas of my life. Especially a toll on my already fragile emotional state, after decades of severe bullying, the death of my father (among others) and my old friend, pain. No matter how hard I tried, I just couldn't lift myself out of the doom cloud surrounding me. I tried CBT, ACT, NLP, and other talking therapies (I have a Psychology degree, so none of this was new), but nothing helped. They failed to shift the anxiety, the depression. If anything, I felt worse because they hadn't helped.

What was wrong with me? Was I doomed to live with this cloud my entire life?

A dear friend came to visit me and told me all about how she had found Reiki while coping with her child's cancer journey. She explained how this had enabled her to lift her emotions, raise her vibration and learn to see the joy buried in the darkness of their current situation. So, I thought I would give this a try. After all, what did I have to lose? If she found it helpful in a situation I deemed far worse than my own, surely it would give me some help. So, I found a local Reiki Master Teacher and went on a course to learn Usui Reiki to practice on myself. Don't get me wrong, this wasn't a cure, but it helped me to understand the importance of energy. It helped ease a little of my pain. It gave me a new outlook on life. It reaffirmed the importance of living life in the higher emotional frequencies. Reiki actually transformed my life so much that I have dedicated years to training. I am now a Reiki Master Practitioner, and I am looking forward to becoming a Reiki Master Teacher in the future.

Back to the start of this chapter, we started looking at emotional vibrations. Even though I still felt all the same symptoms exactly the same as I had before I found Reiki, it allowed me to view my life as if with new glasses. It allowed me to move past just feeling like a collection of symptoms to feeling like a human again. It allowed me to focus on the little positives in my life, not the mountain of negatives. I started to re-frame (as I did with pain) the way I thought. Let me put this into a practical example for you. Rather than say or think "I had a bad day," say or think "There were bad parts to my day, but also good". Even if it was just one good thing and 1000 bad things, focus on that one good thing, not the bad. If you're struggling to find a good part of your day, here are some prompts:

Did you hear the birds sing?
Did you see the beauty of nature—the trees, flowers?
Did you enjoy a hobby—reading, writing, drawing, etc.?
Did you watch one of your favourite TV shows?
Did you see someone you love?

There is always gratitude to be found if we look hard enough. Adopting this allowed me to make more space in my mind for joy, forgiveness, gratitude, peace—all the higher frequency emotions. I am grateful I developed ME/CFS as it gave me a new lease for life. It put me back on my path to help serve others again in a meaningful way to create a better future for us all. A path I had wanted to walk since doing my degree over 15 years ago, but I let life get in the way. My ME/CFS opened me up to the world of Reiki. My ME/CFS gave me time to appreciate all the little beautiful things in my life: a sunset/sunrise, the daily bird chorus, the flowers at my window, cuddles with my fur babies. All of these little moments of gratitude started to build. Once you notice one, the others start to come out of the shadows, and before you know it, you will be able to see joy, peace or gratitude in even the darkest nights of the soul.

I now have my own healing business—Healing with Hannah that works around my symptoms, honouring my body and working with me, not against me. I'm trained and licensed in HeartHealing™, a revolutionary therapy where science meets spirituality in a meditative state. A therapy that is far more powerful than ACT, CBT, NLP or Belief Coding™ in helping to rewrite the narrative in your mind, in helping you to overcome your biggest challenges. A therapy that opens you up to levels of success you may have only dreamed about. This success for me was Healing with Hannah winning an award for inspiring others and becoming a global bestselling author! On a personal level, it allowed me to find the wisdom in my past wounds. I finally felt like I was worthy just as I am. I found a level of self-love I didn't even know was possible after decades of bullying. I finally feel safe to grieve the parts of me that I lost due to ME/CFS.

Rachel Tseng

Founder of Renouvele Body Solutions/Kanna Beast

https://www.instagram.com/thekannabeast
https://www.instagram.com/renouvelebody
http://kannabeast.com
http://renouvelebodycom

Rachel Tseng is the resilient founder of a thriving beauty and wellness clinic, blending science-backed treatments with a deep understanding of inner healing as well as co-founding a athletic supplement and lifestyle brand. Her journey hasn't been easy she navigated the storm of a narcissistic divorce, raised two daughters while attending college full-time, and built a more-than-comfortable life for her three children through sheer grit and grace. A serial entrepreneur at heart, Rachel has launched and grown multiple businesses across industries, each chapter shaping her into a powerful, purpose-driven woman. Her clinic is more than a business it's a reflection of her philosophy that true beauty begins with healing, self-love, and empowerment. Today, Rachel uses her platform to inspire others to rise from hardship, reclaim their worth, and step into abundance inside and out. Her story is a reminder that even in life's messiest seasons, it's possible to build something breathtakingly beautiful.

Ride. Die. Rise

By Rachel Tseng

Piece One: The Raid

"Are you sure you don't know that man who claimed he was just a patient?"

The SWAT officer's voice was sharp, cutting through the static in the air. His eyes scanned my face for cracks, like he was trying to read my soul.

I steadied my voice. "No, officer. I already told you he's just a patient."

He smirked. "Funny. You asked us to hand him your handbag for safekeeping, and he said he doesn't know you. Seems like a bad boyfriend..."

Those words ricocheted in my mind as I sat in the back of the paddy wagon, wrists raw from the cuffs, my knees pressed to my chest. The air smelled like metal, fear, and dust.

This wasn't my first raid, but each one left its mark. This was California's medical marijuana industry during the lawless "cowboy days" before legalization offered safe passage. Back then, it was a dangerous game, and my ex-husband and I were all in.

Piece Two: Survival

We didn't start out in cannabis. We started in real estate. And for a while, we had it all: thriving mortgage business, beautiful home, stability.

Then the market crashed.

Overnight, everything we built was gone. We were drowning two kids, a mountain of bills, and no life raft. Then came his friend with an idea: "Medical marijuana. Legal under California law. We'll make money, help people it's the perfect move."

It sounded almost noble. I've always had a heart for helping others, and the idea of creating safe, regulated access for patients felt right. I wanted to believe we could rebuild.

But what I didn't know was that I was stepping into a cycle of chaos that would test and break pieces of me I didn't even realize existed.

Piece Three: Loyalty

The raids became a rhythm. Sirens, heavy boots pounding across the floor, the metallic click of guns being drawn. "Hands where we can see them!"

Every single time something went wrong, my ex-husband found a way to shift the fallout onto me. And I let him.

Because I was loyal.
Because I believed we were partners.
Because I was the "ride or die" wife.

I wore that title like armor. In truth, it was a leash.

Piece Four: The Wild Years

By then, we had two daughters. I was determined to give them a life of abundance.

We played the perfect family on the outside Sunday Mass at the Catholic church, parent-teacher conferences, volunteering for school events. But at night, our life turned into something out of a movie.

Clubs. VIP tables. Champagne bottles popping. Hundreds of dollars thrown into the air like it was nothing. It was intoxicating. It was distracting.

It was also destructive.

During those years, pieces of me fell away quietly, almost imperceptibly at first. Sleep was a luxury. I survived on alcohol, drugs, and sheer willpower, all while keeping up the appearance of control. I'd go from three hours of sleep to the soccer field, hiding bloodshot eyes behind oversized sunglasses, laughing off the exhaustion.

Friends I had known for years began to slip away. "Things are too crazy," they'd say, sometimes without saying it at all.

Infidelity crept in and became just another unspoken rule of survival brushed aside as "what men do." I told myself love meant forgiveness. In reality, I was disappearing.

Piece Five: The Breaking Point

Eventually, the marriage collapsed. Not quickly, but painfully like a building slowly caving in on itself. The divorce dragged on for seven exhausting years.

By the end, I was financially gutted. But I had my daughters. I had their respect. And I had the broken pieces of myself the parts I would need to rebuild, even if I didn't yet know how.

Piece Six: God and Rebuilding

When I thought there was nothing left of me worth saving, I found love again. I had another child. And I found God.

Getting baptized was more than a spiritual step. It was a symbolic one. The water felt like a washing away of the old life the chaos, the lies I'd told myself, the belief that loyalty meant self-sacrifice.

The pieces of me that I thought were gone forever began returning. Not all at once, and not in their original shape. Therapy, healing courses, self-work they all reshaped me into someone new.

I realized that the woman in the paddy wagon wasn't weak. She was unfinished.

Piece Seven: The New Empire

The empire I'm building now is different.

It isn't built on shaky promises or someone else's version of a dream. It's rooted in healing and empowerment through beauty, wellness, and anti-aging.

It's built by a woman who knows her worth, who knows where loyalty begins and where it ends, and who will never again hand over the keys to her freedom.

The pieces of me are no longer scattered in someone else's chaos. They are mine held together by faith, resilience, and the unshakable truth that I can lose everything and still rise.

Piece Eight: Wholeness

I no longer confuse "ride or die" with love.

I am no longer the woman holding the bag for someone else's mistakes.

I am whole, not because all the pieces are back in place, but because I learned how to make something beautiful out of the broken parts.

And that every messy, painful, powerful piece is me.

JOIN THE MOVEMENT!

#BAUW

Becoming An Unstoppable Woman
With She Rises Studios

She Rises Studios was founded by Hanna Olivas and Adriana Luna Carlos, the mother-daughter duo, in mid-2020 as they saw a need to help empower women worldwide. They are the podcast hosts of the *She Rises Studios Podcast* and Amazon best-selling authors and motivational speakers who travel the world. Hanna and Adriana are the movement creators of #BAUW - Becoming An Unstoppable Woman: The movement has been created to universally impact women of all ages, at whatever stage of life, to overcome insecurities, and adversities, and develop an unstoppable mindset. She Rises Studios educates, celebrates, and empowers women globally.

Looking to Join Us in our Next Anthology or Publish YOUR Own?

She Rises Studios Publishing offers full-service publishing, marketing, book tour, and campaign services. For more information, contact info@sherisesstudios.com

We are always looking for women who want to share their stories and expertise and feature their businesses on our podcasts, in our books, and in our magazines.

SEE WHAT WE DO

OUR PODCAST   **OUR BOOKS**   **OUR SERVICES**

Be featured in the Becoming An Unstoppable Woman magazine, published in 13 countries and sold in all major retailers. Get the visibility you need to LEVEL UP in your business!

Have your own TV show streamed across major platforms like Roku TV, Amazon Fire Stick, Apple TV and more!

Learn to leverage your expertise. Build your online presence and grow your audience with FENIX TV.
https://fenixtv.sherisesstudios.com/

Visit www.SheRisesStudios.com to see how YOU can join the #BAUW movement and help your community to achieve the UNSTOPPABLE mindset.

Have you checked out the *She Rises Studios Podcast?*

Find us on all MAJOR platforms: Spotify, IHeartRadio, Apple Podcasts, Google Podcasts, etc.

Looking to become a sponsor or build a partnership?

Email us at info@sherisesstudios.com